Teenage

YOU DON'T HAVE TO BE PERFECT

You Will Make It!

Tom Krause

Tom Krause

DEDICATION

*To Samuel Thomas Krause
and all teenagers, past, present and future!*

YOU WILL MAKE IT!

Copyright © 2012 Tom Krause

All rights reserved.

ISBN:1718659504
ISBN-13:978-1718659506

Table of Contents

Introduction...

Chapter #1 Be a 7—You Don't Have To Be Perfect...9

Chapter #2 You Will Make It ...20

Chapter #3 I Am Lovable and Capable...28

Chapter #4 Power of Worth...37

Chapter #5 You Will When You Are Ready...48

Chapter #6 You've Got To Get To Twenty-Eight...55

Chapter #7 ABC's of Stress...61

Chapter #8 Sometimes You Just Have To Cry...72

Chapter #9 Building Confidence...80

Chapter #10 Don't Be Afraid to Dream...88

Chapter #11 Choose Your Reactions...98

Chapter #12 Relationships: Can I Trust You?... 105

Chapter #13 Addictions: Keep Your Eyes Open...112

Chapter #14 You Have a Purpose...124

Conclusion...129

About the Author...131

Poetry Index

Seven Is Enough.....18
Heart Of The Soul.....26
Kids By The Wall.....35
Possibilities.....46
Life Is A Work In Progress.....53
Look Forward To The Future.....59
Dare To Believe.....70
Carry On.....78
Get Into The Game.....86
Ode To The Champions.....96
When Life Hands You The Ball.....103
Person That Is Me.....110
Choices.....122
Becoming.....128

Introduction

Teenagers: This book is for you. For almost thirty years I have been a public school teacher. I have also coached numerous athletic teams. Thousands of students have passed through my classroom during my tenure. Over that time I have noticed that teenagers never change. Teens today remain the same wonderful vessels of hope that their parents were three decades ago. What has changed drastically over the years is society's effect on them.

I can remember working on my car when I was a teenager, back in the mid-seventies. It was an old 1966 Ford Mustang six-cylinder. Raising the hood and looking down, I could see the ground. Changing spark plugs was simple.

Fast forward to today. Raise the hood of any car, and you will see a very different sight. A complex maze of wires and parts tells you that this is a complicated machine requiring an expert mechanic.

Life for teenagers today is like that complicated

engine. Society in general has made surviving your teenage years today more complex than it was thirty years ago.

Increasing drug usage, suicide attempts, and high school dropout rates attest to the difficulty many teens face. Because of this environment, I felt the need to write a book designed to help today's teens through the ever-changing fog of puberty.

This book is a compilation of valuable principles I have passed on to teenagers during my years as an educator. The purpose of this book is to provide encouragement and guidance so that you can feel ready to take on life.

Just like thirty years ago, teenagers look in the mirror and ask themselves two questions: "Do I have to be perfect?" and "Will I make it?" The words in this book are meant to help relieve your anxiety and answer those two questions. Many teens over the years have walked up to me after class and said, "Thanks, Coach; I needed to hear that."

I hope you feel the same way when you finish this book.

Teenagers: YOU DON'T HAVE TO BE PERFECT

Chapter 1
You Don't Have To Be Perfect

Teenagers sometimes get too caught up in measuring themselves by the expectations of others. These comparisons can lead to a lot of disappointment when people don't feel like they measure up. When is enough ever good enough?

A young man walked in to his honors history class one Friday morning in late September. He placed his backpack next to his chair, which was located in the back of the room next to the wall.

The young man was a good student, but not a great student. His parents were both professional people—one, a doctor; the other, a lawyer. He was liked by his classmates, though not really well-known because of his shyness.

As the instructor walked into the room, students started removing their history books from their backpacks. Instead of a book, the young man drew out a gun, placed it in his mouth, and pulled the trigger.

Horror, shock, and outrage engulfed the school and the community. Why? How could this happen? Later, people learned that the young man never felt like he lived up to others' expectations. He often spoke of disappointing himself and loved ones.

What a tragedy. Yet I meet many students who tell me that they don't feel "good enough." These feelings lead them to thoughts of dropping out of school, giving up on their dreams, or even worse, suicide.

Letter from Student:

Dear Coach Krause,

My grandma raised me from the time I was born. She was always nagging me about my school work and told me if I didn't get straight As, then I would be a failure. In 5th grade, we moved to a new school district over 2 hours away from my friends. I felt out of place and like no one wanted to be my friend. I would come home, not do my homework, and just communicate with my old friends on the computer. I started getting Fs for grades and my grandma kept telling that I was going to turn out like my mother. I became mad, sad, and depressed. I started doing drugs, and they made me feel better. When my grandma caught me, we had a big argument. I felt like a loser. I then tried to overdose and kill myself. Why? Just like you said in class—sometimes kids are put under so much pressure, they just don't feel like they are good enough.

(The girl in this letter is now off drugs and doing much better.)

Life has a way of heaping higher and higher expectations on today's teens. Unfortunately, adults can get caught up in the comparison game just as easily as teens. And sometimes, parents and guardians are the ones who unconsciously are making teens feel like they aren't good enough.

I once coached a young man named Bobby. Bobby was a great kid with average talent in basketball. Bobby's father, on the other hand, had been a very talented player in high school.

During a junior varsity game one night, Bobby's father sat in the stands continually yelling at his son.

"Bobby, box out!"

"Bobby, shoot!"

"Bobby, pass!"

The constant yelling was not only annoying but also embarrassing.

The next day, I had a conference with Bobby's father.

"What do you think of Bobby?" the father asked.

"Great kid" was my reply.

"If he is such a great kid, then why doesn't he get to play more?" asked the father.

"Let me ask you something," I replied. "When you were playing ball in high school, did your father sit in the stands and yell at you the whole game, telling you what to do?"

"Nobody had to tell me what to do," he said. "I knew what to do. When I played, I just took the ball and did it."

"That's my point," I explained. "Maybe you need to realize your son is not the same player you were in high school. That doesn't make him a bad kid. He may never be as good as you were in basketball, but he is

still a great kid."

Another time, a mother came to me complaining about her daughter. She told me over and over how much her daughter was constantly letting her down— never meeting her expectations.

I finally asked her, "If your daughter grows up to be exactly like you, would that make you happy? "NO!" she said. "I want her to be better than me." "You want her to be better than you?" I replied. "*You* don't even have to be better than you." "What do you mean?" she asked. "When can she ever please you? Your daughter is playing a game she can't win. Maybe she has quit trying."

Dealing with others expectations can be difficult. It is important at this time to really focus in on what you want to do in life. It is fine to listen to advice from others, but it is really important that you make the decisions about your life's future based on your expectations.

Teens tend to react one of three ways to others'

expectations. Below is a brief description of the different roles teens often find themselves fulfilling in response these expectations:

The Golden Teen: **Can do no wrong. Perfect. Never any problems. Star of the team. Feels the pressure of having to remain perfect to keep golden teen status. Overachiever, people pleaser, looks to others for acceptance and status. Worried and nervous.**

The Let-Down Teen: **Can do nothing right. Nothing comes easy. Always has problems. Doesn't even want to play on the team. Always feels like he/she is letting someone down. Can't please others, so doesn't even try. Hates comparisons, especially to the golden teen. Tends to rebel and drop out. Depressed and resentful.**

The Accepted Teen: **Sometimes right, sometimes wrong. Accepts flaws in him/herself and others. May not be the star of the team, but accepts a role in making the team successful. Not afraid to take a chance and fail. Sees him/herself as part of the world. Hopeful and optimistic.**

No matter which type of teenager you feel that you are, in reality, you can live as the Accepted Teen—

you don't have to be perfect, and you don't have to let a few imperfections keep you from doing what you want to do.

When you look into a mirror, what do you see? On a scale of one to ten (one being a total loser and ten being perfect in every way) you should see yourself as a seven.

Seven means you are not perfect but you are OK. Stop looking for a perfect ten in that mirror. Learn to love that seven that you see. In the areas of your life you are really interested in you are probably an eight or nine. In the areas you have no interest in you are probably a five or six. Overall, you are a seven. Seven is a very healthy number. It gives you a little room to be human instead of having to be perfect all the time.

Everyone has faults. Don't let a few faults overshadow your strengths. Pimples aren't permanent and neither is how you feel about yourself today. If you don't always like what you see in the mirror, that's normal. Most people don't like looking into mirrors. Start with a smile and go from there.

Remember, feelings are not facts. Comparing yourself to others is senseless. The thing you have to remember is that you are a unique person with your own strengths and weaknesses. You are an original. There is no one else in the whole world like you, and there never will be. In the world of art, there are many copies of famous paintings and sculptures. The best copies in the world are not nearly as valuable as the originals.

Stop worrying about the things you can't control. Take what you have and make the most of it. Focus on your interests. Find something you like, and go for it.

True motivation comes when people are doing what they want to do versus what they have to do. When people are interested in what they are doing, they don't mind working harder. *The greatest artwork ever created, the greatest invention ever invented, the greatest discovery ever discovered, the greatest song ever written were all accomplished by people who had a passion for their work, not by people who were forced into what they were doing.*

High expectations are fine, but be realistic about what you expect of yourself. When you learn to accept yourself for who you are, life starts falling into place. From there you can grow into your full potential—you may be surprised by what you can accomplish. You don't have to be perfect, just be yourself.

Seven is Enough

When all the world is telling you
to be a perfect ten,
remember there's a better way
to get ahead and win.
The truth is no one's perfect
until they get to heaven—
so wear a smile upon your face
and be a happy seven.
In the things in life you like the most—
that you have interest in—
you probably are an eight or nine,
and some days, even ten!
And for the ones you do not like—
there is no easy fix—
just try to be a four or five,
and maybe even six.
A seven means you've done your best
with everything you've got,
and even if it wasn't great,
you gave it your best shot.
For when you add the numbers up
and total up the sum,
if seven is your average score,
I bet you had more fun.
So put that smile back on your face,
and if life still seems rough,
remember that your Father says
that seven is enough.

Tom Krause

My Journaling

Express your thoughts

Chapter 2
You Will Make It!

Letter from Student

Dear Coach Krause,

I've been going through a lot since moving to my new school. 2 ½ years ago, when I first moved I was devastated and depressed. I became very bitter and angry. Along with depression and suicide attempts came self-destructive cutting and drug usage. I cannot tell you how many times I've attempted suicide, but now I am getting better. I have learned to communicate my feelings, and I am now getting help.

While things are still scary now, I know that someday I will be OK.

I would like to describe the change in teenagers I have seen during my teaching tenure.

Thirty years ago teenagers got picked on at school the way they do today. Name-calling, bullying, and rejection were endured by yesterday's teens as they traveled to adulthood. Teenage suicide, however, was not nearly the problem it is today.

Teenage suicide is now the third leading cause of teenage death.

I recently spoke at a high school assembly attended by over seven hundred students. The first question I asked them was "How many of you know someone who has ever had a suicidal thought?" Almost every one of them raised a hand. That is unacceptable.

Why is teenage suicide such a problem today? What has changed in the last thirty years to raise so many of those hands? Are teenagers today different from teens back then? I don't believe so. I believe the problem is not so much teens', but society's. I think teens today are smarter, brighter and more fun than teens of the past but they are treated worse by society.

While expectations for teens today have risen, support for teens has fallen. Thirty years ago it was easier to feel "normal." I remember the grade I received most in high school was a C. C meant average. It was more acceptable to make a C grade thirty years ago because expectations were different.

Thirty years ago, students went to college because they wanted to, not because they had to. Teens today hear the message that if they don't attend college, then somehow they will not make it in life. Good grades are essential for college admission, so a C grade today is not good enough. Teens today feel pressure to be perfect in order to be successful. Even then they feel they are never good enough. Likewise, in other areas of teenage life today, average is not good enough anymore.

Whether it is appearance, grades, relationships, sports, or other school activities, more teens are feeling the pressure of higher expectations. Add to that the declining family support system today, and teenagers feel overwhelmed.

While teenagers in the past faced expectations and discouragement, they also received acceptance and encouragement for the future.

When I graduated from high school, if you went to college that was great, but if you didn't want to go to college, you simply found a job and started your life. A lot of friends of mine never went to college but went on to live happy successful lives. In reality today, eight out of ten teens today will not graduate from a four year college. That is normal. Yet they still go on to lead happy lives in areas they are interested in.

I once had a student tell me that her whole life people had told her what to wear, how to act, to get good grades, to go to church, etc. She went on to say that no one had ever told her that she would make it, that she was good enough.

Acceptance and encouragement of teenagers has now been replaced by growing expectations and fading hope. Many teens believe that unless they measure up to today's standards, they will never find happiness. As society continues to change, many teenagers have difficulty dealing with who they are, where they belong and who loves them. Feeling overwhelmed, they begin to feel hopeless.

The good news is feelings are not facts. The fact is teenagers today are wonderful. All they need is a little support and encouragement.

Many teens adore their grandparents because they provide just that. Grandparents are often less judgmental. (If you don't have grandparents still living or that you have a good relationship with, think of an older person at church, a neighbor, or a friend's grandparent who appreciates you and treats you with respect.) They tend to be more accepting of teens for who they are.

Many grandparents have a larger perspective on life. They deliver a message of hope that assures today's teens that they will find happiness no matter which path in life they choose.

Grandparents are right. As a teenager today, you are wonderful. You will find happiness. Don't let the negative messages of the world today destroy your future. Be patient. Enjoy being young. When you are older, you will be more ready to take on the world and all its challenges. For now, just do the best you can and give yourself a chance to grow up.

I have taught thousands of teenagers in my career. My message to today's teens: Suicide is not the answer. If you are depressed, seek help. Today, depression is very treatable. There are many resources available through schools, communities, and churches. Don't be too afraid or ashamed to ask. The key is to not suffer alone. If you try one resource and that doesn't work for you, try something else. Don't think that you have to feel this way all the time—you are meant to enjoy life. There is no sense in going through life sad when you have so much to look forward to.

I am very optimistic about the future. Someday today's wonderful teenagers will make this world a better place for all of us. When you get too down on yourself remember, you don't have to be perfect just be yourself and follow your interest. Trust me, You will make it.

The Heart of the Soul

As metal is forged by the fire—
so too is the heart of the soul
made stronger by all of your trials,
as you strive to accomplish your goals.
It's so easy to smile when you're winning,
when fortune is going your way,
but character comes from the struggles
of fighting life's battles each day.
Nothing is real until tested—
you never know what you can do
until, when the odds are against you,
you still find the strength to pull through.
So never back down from the fire
while striving to reach for your goal.
The trials you face on your journey
will strengthen the heart of your soul.

My Journaling

Express your thoughts

CHAPTER 3
I AM LOVABLE AND CAPABLE

I am lovable and capable. I am not perfect. I don't have to be. On a scale of one to ten, I am a seven. I have worth. My worth cannot be measured by a grade point average or a scoreboard. The worth I have comes from the people in this world who love me for me, not for how I look or how I speak, but just for me.

I recognize that others also have worth. Life is not only about me. My purpose in life is to share my gifts and talents with others. My greatest feelings of accomplishment come by giving, not getting.
Through success and failure I remain the same. I am lovable and capable. I have worth. I am accepted for who I am.

Nothing is more important than self-worth. Self-worth is the value that people place on themselves, how they feel about themselves. Worth comes from the feedback that people receive from others and the feedback they give themselves during self-talk.

Self-talk is the "tape" that you play in your head during the day. For example, when you answer a question incorrectly in class, you might think *Why did I say something that stupid?* or something more positive like *Oh well, I'll get it next time*. Either way, your self-talk is a major contributor to your sense of self-worth.

What makes self-worth so important is that if a person doesn't feel he is worth anything, he will never try anything. If a person never tries anything, he can't get the confidence boost he needs to try other things.

I am the father of two rowdy red-headed boys. Sometimes they irritate me; sometimes they make messes, but no matter how much trouble they cause, they are still my sons. They are not perfect and don't have to be to have my love. They are simply accepted.

The same applies to you. As you grow, you will make mistakes. You will let yourself and others down. But that doesn't take away your value. In God's eyes you are accepted the way you are and you can do amazing things.

We all need to realize the power we possess to

make another human being feel worth.

Imagine a young man who is a freshman in high school. It is the first day of school. It is also his first day in a brand new high school after moving to the district with his mother.

He gets up in the morning, looks in the mirror, combs his hair, and goes downstairs to eat breakfast. As he walks out the door to meet the bus, his mother gives him a kiss and says, "Have a great day at school, son."

While attempting to get on the bus, the boy trips and falls. Kids on the bus laugh. It is not a big deal, but he is embarrassed, and a little bit of his self-worth is torn away.

Upon entering the bus, he hurries to find a seat. As he starts to sit down, he hears, "I'm not sitting by you. Move on." It is no big deal, but another little bit of his self-worth is torn away.

After arriving at the school, he stands by his locker before the first bell and sees all the other students talking with their friends. He is overwhelmed by the size of his new school because he came from a very small district. He wonders how he will meet friends at this great big school. He doubts himself. No big deal, but another little piece of his self-worth is torn away.

As he sits in his first hour class, the teacher asks a question. He thinks he knows the answer, so he raises his hand. When called upon, he blurts out an answer that is not even close to being right. Someone in the class snickers.

After class he walks into the hallway and stands next to some of the students from the class. He doesn't say anything, just stands there listening. One of the other students sees him and says, "What are you doing, eavesdropping?" No big deal, but a little more of his self-worth is torn away.

It is lunchtime. As he goes through the lunch line, he remembers the names he was called at his old school for being overweight. He doesn't want to hear those names at his new school, so when he goes through the line he doesn't get the kind of lunch he wants to eat. He leaves the lunchroom hungry. It is not a big deal, but a little more of his self-worth is torn away.

He likes music. As he sits in music class singing loudly, he thinks he sees other students staring at him. He stops singing. It is not a big deal, but a little more of his self-worth is torn away.

On his way home someone on the bus calls him a name. As he leaves the bus and walks to his house, his mother meets him on the steps. "Did you have a good day at school?" she asks. He feels like a loser, but you can't explain that to your mother, so he mumbles as he walks by her and goes to his bedroom. For most of that evening, he stays in his room trying to heal up from his first day at school.

The next morning, he gets up and doesn't like what he sees when he looks in the mirror to comb his hair for school. As he walks past his mom she says, "Honey, have a good day at school." He already knows what his day at school will be like. He is not going to answer any tough questions, try to meet new people, or get involved in any activities. Why? He can't keep losing. He knows that. He is just going to protect what little self-worth he has left. He is not going to try.

When people don't feel they are worth anything, they don't try anything. When they don't try anything they can't get the confidence they need to try other things. Eventually they begin to feel worthless.

How long does it take for us to say "hi!" to others in the hallways of school? That little bit of recognition might just be enough to brighten someone's day. I have learned that if a student in my class feels that I like them – they try. Trying is the start of growing.

Maybe that is why I react strongly to bullying. There is never a time to diminish a person's feelings of worth just because you have power over someone. Your power is better spent building up than tearing down. That is the power of worth.

KID BY THE WALL

He stands all alone
just a kid by the wall
as others pass by
on their way through the hall.

He never does talk –
just waits for his class.
not daring to speak
unless he is asked.

Meeting new friends –
how hard will he try?
He would like to reach out
but he is lonely and shy.

I you want to help
in a very small way
a simple "hello"
is all you need say.

But if nobody cares
as they pass in the hall,
he will always remain
just a kid by the wall.

Tom Krause

My Journaling

Express your thoughts

Chapter 4
The Power of Worth

The older I get, the clearer this simple truth becomes – *People Count – People Matter. People make a difference!*

One semester I had a student who always seemed hyperactive in class. He was unable to concentrate. In the hallways in school he was constantly getting in trouble. Other students bumping into him would immediately send him into a rage, and he found himself in numerous altercations. Whenever we discussed teenage issues, he would raise his hand and give very insightful opinions. Whenever I asked him to do any homework, he never turned in anything.

At the end of the grading quarter I asked him how his grades were in all his classes. "I haven't passed anything since I started high school," He said.

"Really?" I replied. "How come? You seem like a pretty smart kid to me."

He went on to tell me that in junior high he was on the Principal's Honor Roll. At that time he lived with his grandparents. His grandfather would take him fishing and to football games. His grandmother would cook for him and tell him stories. He truly experienced a home full of love.

At the end of his eighth-grade year, however, his grandfather passed away. Since his grandmother was growing too old to raise a teenage boy, he was sent to live with his parents. His parents were divorced and living in two different towns.

First, he was sent to live with his mom. She would work all day then go out all night. She really didn't want him. Then he was sent to live with his father. Same story – his father would work all day then go out all night. He really didn't want his son either.

The young man went on to tell me that in the two years since he had left his grandparents house he had changed schools 13 times.

At the end of that school year – just two years after he'd been on the Principal's Honor Roll - the young man dropped out of school with zero credits. The two years he spent in high school, he was always looked on as a "bad kid". Maybe he wasn't such a "bad kid". Maybe he just needed a home.

Never underestimate the power of the human connection on the success or failure of other humans in our society.

Donald Jenry came out for basketball at our school during his eighth grade year. This is remarkable because Donald suffered from cystic fibrosis, a terminal disease that caused fluid to build up in his lungs. Because of this disease, Donald was very limited in what he could do on the court. As a matter of fact, Donald could barely run from one end of the court to the other without bending over and coughing to clear his lungs. Sometimes his cough was so severe his face would turn blue as he gasped for air.

I kept Donald on the team, playing him sparingly at the end of each game. Every time he went in, all our fans would give him a standing ovation. Even though he would have to come out after one trip up and down the floor, he inspired the whole gym.

One day in practice as we were preparing to run conditioning drills, I noticed Donald severely coughing at the end of the gym. Concerned, I walked over to him and said, "Donald, you don't have to run these drills."

"What?" he replied.

"Just sit out. It's okay," I told him.

"NO!" he said emphatically. "I'm making myself better for the team."

From then on I started using Donald differently during the games. Instead of playing him at the end of the game when it didn't matter. I played him when it mattered most. Any time the team needed a boost – in came Donald. Every time his exit was followed by cheers from his teammates as well as our fans. His presence had a way of firing up our players at times when they needed it most.

At the end of that school year, Donald lost his battle with cystic fibrosis. At his funeral his teammates and I gathered to pay our last respects. Even though Donald was extremely limited when it came to physical ability, he was unanimously chosen the Most Valuable Player of the team.

I once taught a girl named Tina who was born with cerebral palsy. Because of a lack of oxygen to the brain at birth, Tina's muscles were very stiff at birth.

With the help of her family, especially her grandfather who would physically massage her muscles daily, Tina was able to start kindergarten on time with the help of a wheelchair. She couldn't speak, however, until third grade because of the stiffness of her facial muscles. Through hard work, Tina was able to leave her wheelchair behind and go to middle school on a walker.

Tina's whole life she was different from the rest of the students. It wasn't her fault - she was born that way. Because of her differences, she was sometimes picked on by the other students in school. If anyone had reason to pout or be negative about life, Tina did. But that was not her. She always wore a big smile that reflected the joy in her heart.

I first met Tina when she was seventeen years old walking down the hallways of school on her walker between classes. What caused me to notice her was the way she would take her walker and purposely run into good-looking boys in the hallway. She would then flash her big smile and say, "Hi!" Tina Larsen was seventeen years old and boy crazy.

One day I gave an assignment to my class that involved memorizing a poem entitled, "Don't Quit". I explained that each student whose name I called out was to stand and recite one of the three verses of the poem. Those who could recite all three verses would get bonus points. As I looked around the room, I noticed Tina's usually big smile was gone. She looked worried and concerned. I quickly announced the assignment was worth ten points.

The bell to end class rang, and as the students filed out, I noticed Tina still worried about the assignment. "Tina," I said, "Don't worry about it. The assignment is only worth ten points." My words didn't seem to help as she made her way out of my room.

The next day in class as I called out the first name in my grade book to recite the poem, I was met with a surprise.

"Sorry! I forgot to do the assignment," was the student's response. "But it was only worth ten points, right?"

I then call on the next name and got pretty much the same response.

"Sorry, but I had a game last night," was the next response. "But it was only worth ten points, right?" I soon discovered that every time I called a name the response was the same. They had all just ignored the assignment because it wasn't worth very many points. Finally, in frustration and half kidding, I proclaimed that the next person who didn't recite the poem perfectly had to drop on the floor and give me ten push-ups. This was a leftover discipline technique from my days as a physical education teacher.

To my surprise, Tina was next. Tina used her walker to move to the front of the class and, straining to form the words, began to try to recite the poem. She made it to the end of the first stanza when she made a mistake. Before I could say a word, she threw her walker to the side, fell to the floor and started doing push-ups.

I was horrified and wanted to say, "Tina, I was just kidding!" But she crawled back up in her walker, stood in front of the class and continued the poem. She finished all three stanzas perfectly, one of only a handful of students who did, as it turned out.

When she finished, a fellow student spoke up

and asked, "Tina, why did you do that? It's only worth ten points!"

Tina took her time forming the words and said, "Because I wanted to be like you guys - normal."

Silence fell on the whole room when another student exclaimed, "Tina, we're not normal, we're teenagers! We get in trouble all the time."

"I know," Tina said as a big smile spread across her face.

Tina got her ten points that day in class. She also got the love and respect of her classmates. To her, that was worth a whole lot more than ten points.

From that day forward Tina's acceptance and popularity grew. At the height of her popularity her senior year, Tina was selected homecoming queen during the football season. Instead of feeling "different" from her classmates, Tina at last felt "special".

Donald and Tina are two examples of the power of worth. When people feel self-worth, they try. They refuse to be victims in life because they know that people believe in them, and they believe in themselves.

Possibilities

When your dreams start to seem so impossible—
when roadblocks are all you can see—
look beyond all the problems that face you
and focus on possibilities.
Don't limit your thoughts to the present
or solutions you have learned from the past.
Remember to keep looking forward—
you may find the answer at last.
It is you who determines your future—
how your journey through tomorrow will be.
To fill all your days with adventure,
dare to see what no one else dares to see.
So never let obstacles stop you—
or keep you from doing your part.
Have faith that your dreams are all possible
if you truly believe in your heart.

My Journaling

Express your thoughts

Chapter 5
You Will When You're Ready

I once taught elementary school, grades one through five. One of the activities we would do in class was a relay race. I noticed that when I asked the first graders to skip during a race, a number of boys were unable to do so. While all of the girls could skip, some of the boys could never grasp the concept and trotted instead. I asked a veteran teacher at the time why boys in first grade could not skip? Her answer enlightened me, "Because they are not ready to skip. Give them time to grow and mature and they will skip just like the girls."

By the time the same boys got to third grade, skipping was not a problem. They all could do it easily.

I was approached about giving a grade to my first grade students. I was told to assign a grade for skipping, which I refused to do. "What about the boys who can't skip?" I asked. "What kind of grade do I give them?"

"If they can't do it, then they get an F for that

activity," I was told.

An "F"? Why would I give a little boy an F for something he is just not ready to do? By third grade, little boys forget all about not being able to skip in first grade. But if you give them an F, they may never try again.

Sometimes we judge ourselves too early. Just because you are struggling with something today, doesn't mean you will always struggle. Give yourself more time. You don't have to be ready for everything all at once, but when you are ready, you'll find success.

My ten-year-old stepson loves to play football. All he talks about is how someday he will be in the NFL. The look of enthusiasm on his face during his mighty mite football games reveals his excitement.

If I took him at ten-years-old and put him in a game against high school players, he would get killed. The game would be too hard. Before long he would hate football because there would be no chance to win. Someday he might be a great high school player, but at ten, he is simply not ready.

When I was in high school, I struggled with

math. If I had taken geometry as a sophomore, I would have flunked it. Instead, I waited until I was a senior to take geometry. Because I waited till I was more mature, more ready, I passed geometry my senior year.

Sometimes teens measure themselves as successes and failures too early in life. What may seem impossible for you now may become a reality for you later. Give yourself a chance to grow. You deserve a chance at success just like anyone else.

One of my favorite stories is of a father and son who went into the woods to chop down a tree. The father carried an axe. The son carried a hatchet. When they came across a large tree, the little boy ran to the tree and started hitting it with his hatchet. The hatchet barely made a dent in the trunk of the tree. The father said, "Stand back, son." The father then began chopping the tree with the axe. Finally, the tree fell to the ground, and the father instructed the son to use his hatchet to chop off the smaller branches.

A few years later, the father and son went back into the woods to once again chop down a tree. This time, upon finding a large tree, the son grabbed the axe from his father and said, "Let me do it, Dad." Because the axe was heavy, the son could only swing it five or six times before his arms grew weary. At that point, the father took back the axe and finished chopping down the tree. He then instructed his son to again take the hatchet and chop off the smaller branches.

Years passed, and one last time the father and son went to chop down a tree. This time, when they came to a large tree, the son took the axe from his father and chopped the tree until it fell to the ground.

When the tree hit the ground, the son knew he was a man.

If you are struggling with something right now, don't give up. Don't see yourself as a failure. Give yourself more time to grow stronger. Keep going back to that tree and swinging the axe. When you are ready, that tree will fall.

Nature teaches us that flowers bloom when they are ready and not before. It is the same with you. It is hard to be patient but know that your time to bloom is coming. When it does, you will do amazing things.

Life Is A Work In Progress

Life is a work in progress
that never is complete.
We learn a different lesson
from each experience we meet.

We learn the joy of living -
of what a heart is for.
We learn that through our struggles
We are stronger than before.

We learn the thrill of victory –
the pain of a defeat.
We learn to win the battle
We must first learn to compete.

We learn from our reactions
to the things we can't control-
there are times we should hang in there
and times we should let go.

These lessons that we gather
as we travel on our way-
help complete our work in progress –
a fulfilled life someday.

Tom Krause

My Journaling

Express your thoughts

Chapter 6
You've Got to Get to Twenty-Eight

It is easy to get caught up in the problems of today. For most teenagers high school seems as though it will last forever. In reality, high school is just ten minutes out of your whole life. While your time in school is important, it is really only a small part of the total picture. The best part of your life begins after high school.

When I was in high school, there was a girl in school named Sarah, who was by far the prettiest girl in school. All of us boys drooled when she walked into the classroom. We paid very little attention to the rest of the girls in class when Sarah was around. We always thought, "If I could only marry Sarah—life would be perfect." Not that we would ever have a chance to marry Sarah, or even date her, for that matter. No, Sarah dated older guys. But we didn't mind. Just the thought of her was enough to keep our minds occupied as we suffered through the boring days of school.

Ten years after we graduated, we all gathered at our high school reunion to reacquaint ourselves with former classmates. Word soon spread that Sarah had arrived. Excited, my friends and I lined up, hoping to get the first glimpse of the former beauty. We were stunned.

As Sarah walked by, it was obvious that the girl of our dreams had changed. The beauty we had once admired was now hidden by excessive weight and wrinkled clothes. Her personality (which was never that great to begin with) had changed from arrogant to mean. It was frightening to think that if we had gotten what we dreamed about ten years before, this would have been our reality.

Suddenly, I noticed a very attractive woman making her way through the crowd toward me. I was surprised when she walked up to me and began talking as if we had known each other for a long time. The whole time I was talking with her I couldn't figure out who she was.

When she moved on to speak to someone else, I asked a fellow classmate if he recognized her. To my amazement, she was a classmate whom I'd sat next to many times during high school.

People change. Students often assume that the rest of their lives will be just like high school. Not true. The years between graduation and their ten-year high school reunion are a time of great change for most people.

I often tell my students, "The best time of your life is when you are twenty-eight-years-old. When you are twenty-eight, you can live anywhere, be anything, and act any way you choose." High school isn't real life. Real life begins after high school. High school is like batting practice. The real game begins when you get out.

Don't get so hung up in the problems of today that you stop looking forward to your future. You are not going to be a teenager forever. You are going to continue to grow and change.

By the time you turn twenty-eight, the freedom to make your own decisions in life, right or wrong, will give you a feeling of empowerment in your own life. With each experience, confidence and self assurance will grow until you feel completely like yourself. It is truly an awesome time of life. Don't do something in high school to keep you from experiencing it.

Deal with today, but keep hope alive for tomorrow. You will never regret it. Remember, who you become is totally up to you. Your best days are ahead of you. When things start to seem hopeless, focus your thoughts on twenty-eight.

Look Forward to Your Future

Look forward to your future—
don't hang on to the past.
Dare to open up your heart
to find your dreams at last.
Though it sometimes seems so scary
to walk in faith each day—
if you really want to learn to live,
it is the only way.
What good is claiming to have trust
in God's ultimate plan
if you refuse to place your life
into the Master's hands?
So learn to face each day with hope,
though it may take awhile.
It is in your future—not your past—
that you will find your smile.

Tom Krause

My Journaling

Express your thoughts

Chapter 7
ABCs of Stress

Feeling tired a lot? Do you have headaches and sleep issues? If so you may be suffering from a common teenage condition called TOO MUCH STRESS!!!

Homework, extracurricular activities, grade expectations, relationship issues are all examples of how many stressors students deal with during a normal day. Teens often begin to feel overwhelmed with worry which leads to many of the symptoms listed above.

One of the main symptoms of stress is fatigue. There are three types of fatigue. Physical fatigue caused by physical activity can be cured with rest. Physiological fatigue caused by a germ or virus can be cured with medicine and rest. Psychological fatigue, however, is caused by worry and cannot be cured by rest. You could sleep for five days and still feel a lack of energy if worry still occupies your thoughts.

Below are some helpful tips to lighten your worry

load and help you feel like your old self again.

(A) Avoid Perfectionism

My grandfather was a house painter. In his lifetime he must have painted hundreds of houses, inside and out. He was a happy, outgoing man who made friends easily. It wasn't hard to tell that he loved his work as well as his life. He was also an excellent painter. No one could paint a wall like Grandpa. Consequently, he was always in demand.

Once, while in college, I went to help Grandpa paint a house. While working inside, I noticed how skilled he was at quickly giving a wall a quality coat of paint. As a matter of fact, he could carry on a conversation with the homeowner, laughing all the time, while painting three walls to my one.

At one point, he stopped to watch me. He noticed how I took my time dipping the brush in the paint bucket and how I carefully wiped off both sides of the brush as I pulled it out in order not to waste any paint. I then spread a thin coat of paint on the wall without spilling a drop. It was a slow, tedious process, but I dared not laugh or "kid around" for fear of making a mess.

Finally, he offered me some advice. "Here, watch this," he said, as he took the brush from my hand. Dipping the it deep into the bucket, he then produced a brush dripping with paint. "See," he said. "This is how you do it. Don't worry about spills and messes. They can always be cleaned up. Treat a wall the way you treat people—be generous. Have fun. Always put enough paint on the brush."

With that he turned and applied a thick coat of paint to the wall while at the same time resuming his conversation with the homeowner. Yes, he did spill a few drops, but I noticed how much better his wall looked than mine. I also noticed how much fun he was having.

I've always remembered the "painting advice" my grandfather gave me that day. Life is not always perfect. Some days we spill very few drops. Some days we spill a lot. The only thing that really matters is what the wall looks like when we are done (and how much fun we had painting it).

(B) Be Prepared

Feeling unorganized is very stressful. In order to relieve that stress I have three suggestions. (1) Plan, (2) Stick to the plan, and (3) Have a back up plan.

Plan. When I was in college I followed a simple plan that helped me get through school. From the time of my last class on Friday till Sunday night at 7 p.m. was my free time. I tried to use that time just for me to do anything I wanted. Sunday night at 7 p.m. I would sit down at my desk and organize my week. I would write out what I had scheduled for each day of the week, from homework to sports practice. That simple bit of organization helped keep me on track and reduced my stress.

Stick to the plan. There is nothing more stressful than to keep changing your mind, constantly coming up with a new plan to follow. Once you have decided on a direction, stick with it until outcomes dictate a change.

In coaching I use to set up my teams strategy based on the strengths of my players. Watching other teams it was always tempting to do what they were doing, but it never worked. The more we stuck to the game plan based on our personnel, the more success we had.

Always have a back-up plan. When I was coaching basketball, I used an out-of-bounds play called "Bubble." It was a simple play designed to get the ball back inbounds during crucial situations. I had learned over the years that one of the most stressful moments of a game was trying to inbound the ball while the other team was applying full court pressure, trying to steal the ball back. I would have my team practice the "Bubble," but we never used it in a game unless our normal play to inbound wasn't working. Many games were won using that simple back-up plan. It allowed us to make a stressful situation less stressful because we were prepared. Murphy's Law says "That which can go wrong will... at the worst possible moment." Knowing ahead of time what to do in case your plan goes awry alleviates worry.

(C) Create Space

People need space. Space away from their worries. The more stress you are under, the more space you require. If you don't think space plays a factor in stress, try going to the mall at Christmas time. Fighting all the crowds shopping in the stores wears you out and raises your anxiety level—all you want to do is go find a quiet place to rest in.

In my hometown of Boonville, MO, there is an old Indian burial mound that sits high atop the Missouri River bluffs. From that mound, looking down on the river bottoms, one can see for miles. I use to like to go there as a kid and just sit and enjoy the view. It was so quiet and peaceful up there. Watching those river bottoms below helped keep things in perspective for me.

If you feel like life is closing in on you, create space. Find you own special place that gives you a chance to find peace. Go for a walk, a drive in the country— anything to get away from your worries.

Sometimes you even need a break from your best friends. Space gives you time to sort things out and get a perspective on your problems.

(D) Don't Overbook Yourself

A common complaint I hear from teenagers is "I HAVE TOO MUCH TO DO AND NOT ENOUGH

TIME TO DO IT!" My word of advice to you is learn to say the word "NO."

A common myth today is that the busier you are, the more you stay out of trouble. The problem with that idea is that every commitment you make comes with its own set of expectations. This causes stress. Remember, there are many excellent activities to get involved in during high school, but there are only so many hours in the day and only one of you. Your body and brain need free time just to rest, recover, and reenergize. Learning to say "NO" keeps you from overbooking and spreading yourself too thin.

(E) Eat, Exercise & Sleep Enough

Just as a car requires gas to keep running, so your body needs food for energy. In today's fast paced world, it is easy to skip meals. Some teens believe that skipping meals helps them lose weight. In the long run, skipping meals does the complete opposite.

Skipping meals not only slows down your metabolism, which makes you burn calories slower and gain weight faster, it drains you of energy. If your plan is to lose weight, eat smaller portions more often throughout the day and add physical activity to your daily routine. You cannot starve yourself into a new body, but you can change your body the healthy way and improve your energy level as well.

Exercise not only burns calories, it also reduces stress. Don't confuse exercise with training for a sport. Athletes are put through training when preparing for a sport season. Exercise should be more personalized for you and your needs.

Anyone can exercise. Swimming, jogging, riding a bike are great ways to add activity to your day. Your exercise routine may be as simple as walking with a friend or parent. Exercise can also be done alone with your headset. Whatever you choose, pick an activity that you enjoy. The benefits of less stress and more energy will amaze you.

Along with eating well and exercise, getting enough sleep is crucial to reducing stress. Sleep is your body's way of recharging itself. Many teens today have sleeping issues because of stress. Letting go of thoughts and worries in order to fall asleep can be hard. Some people listen to music at bedtime as a way to take their mind off things and fall asleep. Others leave a fan or a television on to distract themselves from their thoughts.

Whatever techniques you use to reduce stress, always keep in mind that there is nothing more important than your health and happiness. Be nice to yourself—you deserve it!

Dare To Believe

If you dare to believe -
to follow your star...

If you seek out your purpose
to find out who you are...

If you call on your courage
to find hope in your heart...

If you challenge your
talent to fulfill its part...

If troubles and setbacks
cannot stand in your way...

If you find the resolve
to live life everyday...

Then what you will find
at the end of the road

Is strength in your heart
and peace in your soul.

My Journaling

Express your thoughts

_____
_____
_____
_____
_____
_____
_____
_____
_____
_____
_____
_____
_____
_____
_____
_____
_____
_____
_____
_____

Chapter 8
Sometimes You Just Have to Cry

Three things everyone needs to learn about emotions are:

1. Emotions are normal. To feel happy, sad, excited, or mad is perfectly normal.

2. Feelings are not facts. Emotions are like the weather—they change. Today is cloudy. Tomorrow might be sunny. Just because you feel lousy doesn't mean you are lousy. This is just a temporary feeling that can change at any time.

3. Expression is the opposite of depression. Finding healthy ways to express emotions is a key to good mental health. Holding emotions in too long is not good. Suppressing emotions can lead to depression.

About two months into parenthood, I learned the true meaning of the word *heartbreak*. There could not have been anything worse than watching helplessly as my son received his first round of immunization shots.

I would have rather have been run over by a truck than have to sit there and watch him go through that. While listening to his screams, I kept thinking that surely medical science could have come up with a better way of doing this by now. As for any sympathy from the doctor, all he could say was, "Ah—look at those healthy tears."

As we left the office, I whispered into my son's ear, "It's okay, Sam. Sometimes you just have to cry."

I guess it was only a matter of time before my son was introduced to pain in his life. Later, when he was three-years-old, he fell face-first down a steep hill. As he sat on the ground crying, I tried to comfort him while at the same time wiping the blood from his scrapes. While some people believe that little boys should not cry, I contend that if you can't cry when you are three-years-old, when can you cry?

Crying is the expression of a healthy human emotion. When people are sad or in pain, one method of expressing that emotion is by crying. What's wrong with that? I agree children shouldn't cry for the wrong reasons, but there are times when even adults need to cry.

After my father's sudden death many years ago, I tried to remain strong. For about a month, I walked around stoic—determined not to show weakness.

One day a song came on the radio that reminded me of him. I completely lost it. It was the first time since the funeral that I just let go and cried. It felt good not to hold back. I loved my father very much. Crying for him didn't make me less of a man. It just made me more of a son.

There will be times in my son's life when he will feel pain. When that happens, I hope I am there for him. If I am not, I hope he remembers the words I whispered in his ear that day as we left the doctor's office: "It's okay, Sam. Sometimes you just have to cry."

Anger is another emotion that is misunderstood. Anger comes from frustration. Anger is a way of standing up for yourself. I tell athletes all the time, "If I can't make you angry—I can't coach you." Anger just means you care.

I once coached a point guard in basketball whom

I loved. He was very competitive and a true leader on the floor. One night, during a game, he stole a pass and dribbled the length of the floor for a game tying lay-up. When the shot didn't go in, he ran out of bounds and slammed his fist against the wall, breaking his hand. It wasn't his frustration I objected to, it was that he expressed it in a way that hurt him and the rest of the team.

Learning to express anger is essential if you want to get along with people. People are frustrating. Anger can be expressed in many ways that don't lead to harm. Some people run; some people scream; some people write it all down, and then throw it away. Whichever method they choose, the fact that they are able to get their anger out is healthy.

Like anger, fear is a very powerful emotion that has a huge effect on people's lives. Everyone has fear. People who say they have no fear are either lying or not normal. A little fear is a good thing. It is fear that keeps us from going places or doing things that may be harmful to us. Too much fear, on the other hand, can hold us back when we need to step forward.

Fear paralyzes people at times. "I would like to go to college, but I'm afraid I can't do it." "I would like to see the world, but I am afraid to fly." These are statements that indicate fear is holding a person back from having a fulfilled life.

Young men sometimes mistakenly equate fear with cowardice. They think that, just because they are afraid, they are cowards. In reality, courage cannot exist without fear. Courage is not the absence of fear. Courage is being afraid and acting anyway. If you are not afraid to do something, it takes no courage to do it. But if you are afraid to ask the pretty girl out and you still do it—that takes guts.

Emotions sometimes make teens feel like they are not normal. That is not the case. Good mental health involves feeling good about self, getting along with others, and meeting the demands of life. Those three areas of your life don't always have to be perfect. There are days we like ourselves and others more than other days. There are also some days we feel the frustration of not getting much done. That is normal.

Whatever emotions you are dealing with, remember:

Feelings are not facts. Emotions are normal. Learning to deal with emotions is part of becoming a mature human being.

Carry On

At times when you feel troubled,
when your happiness is gone,
look to the heart within you
for the strength to carry on.
In your heart you will find special virtues,
such as faith and hope and love.
These gifts have been sent down to you
from a Power up above.
It is faith that keeps the soul searching
for the joy the heart hopes for.
It is love that heals the spirit,
making it stronger than before.
And if your heart be broken,
if your strength should fade away,
the power of these virtues
will still win on that day.
So remember when you're troubled,
when happiness is gone,
look to the heart within you
for the strength to carry on.

My Journaling

Express your thoughts

Chapter 9
Building Confidence

Confidence comes when people do things they have never done before. When people overcome obstacles in life, their confidence levels start to grow.

Watch how an infant gains confidence as he grows from crawling to walking. The look on his face tells the whole story of how he feels about his accomplishments. This success leads the toddler to overcome other obstacles during his developmental stages. The same principle continues for the rest of the child's life—success leads
to success.

When I first met my stepson, Tyler, he was four years old. He loved to ride his bike. He would zoom up and down the street like a little speed demon.

One day I announced it was time to take his training wheels off the bike so he could learn to ride without them. Immediately he protested.

"NO! I can't ride my bike without them!" he exclaimed.

"I think you can" was my reply.

"NO!" he continued to protest.

With the training wheels off, I coaxed him into sitting on his bike as I stood next to him, assuring him that he would not fall. I then took one step away and promised to catch him if he tried to ride to me.

After he successfully rode that far, I then took two steps from him and urged him to try again. Once again he successfully rode to me without falling.

I continued to take steps back, adding to the distance of the trial, and he continued to be successful in riding to me without falling. Soon he was riding up and down the street on his own without the aid of training wheels. His reaction spoke volumes.

"Go tell Mom to come watch me!" Tyler shouted.

"Look, Mom! I'm doing it!" he proudly announced, as he displayed his newfound ability.

Sometimes, the greater the obstacle you overcome, the greater the confidence you gain.

One of the greatest teachers I had in high school was my football coach. I remember one particular night during a junior varsity football game, our coach taught us a lesson we would never forget.

Coach's favorite play was called 37X. It was a simple handoff to the fullback over the left tackle. Nothing fancy—just basic football, but for some reason it was the first play we ran every game. When we took the huddle that night, we already knew what play to run first—37X. As we broke the huddle, however, we were greeted with a sight that spelled certain doom for coach's favorite play. There, lined up right over our left tackle was the biggest junior varsity player we had ever seen. He was huge, nearly 300 lbs. and very intimidating. As the play unfolded, our fullback ran right into the gigantic defensive lineman and was tackled for no gain. It was like running into a brick wall. Disgusted, our fullback picked himself up and staggered back to the huddle. We knew right away that coach had better run a different play.

As the wide receiver came from the side of the field, he ran up to the quarterback and said, "Coach said run

37X again." The results were the same.

Our next three offensive possessions were the same. Each play, we ran 37X and punted. Finally our coach's stubbornness paid off. On the first play of our fourth possession, 37X went for a huge gain all the way down to the eight-yard line. On first and goal from the eight, our wide receiver ran onto the field with the next play. Our quarterback ignored him, saying, "We know—37X." "No, no!" yelled the receiver. "Coach said run any play you want to run." "What?" said the quarterback? "Coach said run any play you want to run," the receiver again replied. Amazed, the quarterback turned to us and said, "Linemen, what do you want to run?" "37X!" was our loud reply. The result, TOUCHDOWN!

Our coach always used to say, "Never run away from what you are afraid of—run right at it."

We rarely forget those moments in our lives when confidence is born. We remember those who first taught us to ride a bike, solve a problem, or read a book. We remember the moments the light bulbs lit up in our minds and we suddenly realized, "I can do it!"

Those special moments help us believe in

ourselves enough to try other things—to accept more challenges and grow to become confident adults, not giving in to the fear of failure. As success leads to more success, confidence grows from the inside out.

When you were a toddler learning to walk you fell down a lot. But each time you got back up on your feet until you mastered walking. After that running and climbing were things you conquered. Every time you fell as a toddle you didn't judge yourself, you simply tried again until you succeeded. That is how winning is done!

Never be afraid of failure. Always start at the bottom and work your way to the top one step at a time. The confidence you gain and the experience you acquire is what will keep you on top once you get there. If you happen to fail from time to time, don't give up. Keep building on your positive past until you reach your dreams.

Get into the Game

Standing on the sidelines
isn't quite the same.
To live a life worth living,
you've got to get into the game.
Looking toward the future,
trying to prepare,
waiting for your turn to play
doesn't always seem quite fair.
But the will to be a winner
won't accept the words "I quit."
It makes you keep on trying
when others choose to sit.
And finally, when you're ready,
when life gives you a chance,
you find the joy of living
when you step into the dance.
Standing on the sidelines
isn't quite the same.
To live a life worth living,
get into the game.

Tom Krause

My Journaling

Express your thoughts

Chapter 10
Don't be Afraid to Dream

Suppose I took a group of people into a dark gymnasium and asked them all to stand by one wall while I placed a small, unlit birthday candle by the opposite wall and then instructed them to find the candle. Someone might find the candle by accident, but most would wander around helplessly in the dark.

Now, imagine I lit the candle and again asked the group to find the candle. The whole group could follow the little flame through that vast darkness and walk right to the candle with no problem.

Goals are like candles lit in the dark. Goals give people a sense of direction in life. They provide a purpose and a hope for the future. They keep people from wandering around blindly in life. When you accomplish a goal, you achieve a feeling of confidence.

If goals are so important, then why do so many people shy away from them? One reason is fear of failure. People fear that if they set a goal and don't achieve it, then they have failed. Failure is not the end.

Quitting is the end. Failing just means you are trying the wrong way. If you truly believe in your goal, find a way to change direction and get back on course.

Courage is not the absence of fear. Courage is being afraid and doing it anyway. Courage is facing fear and running right through it. Behind fear is freedom. One never finds freedom by running away. Don't let fear paralyze you. Don't let it keep you from chasing goals that would truly make you happy.

THE CARD STORY

I remember how I felt when the idea hit me, thrilled, certain and ready! It was in algebra class, the spring of my junior year. Football season was long over, and the next season was a long way away. We had done well that year, qualifying for the playoffs for the first time in school history, and I wanted us to do even better the next year, 1974, my senior year.

But how? Then the idea hit me. I didn't wait until after school. During my lunch break, I drove over to a print shop and ordered business cards with a simple, direct prophecy –

"BOONVILLE PIRATES 1974 STATE CHAMPIONS"

When the cards were printed, my teammates and I distributed them all over town. Teachers pinned them to classroom bulletin boards. Merchants taped them in store windows. Pretty soon those cards were everywhere. There was no escaping them, and that's what we wanted. We wanted our goal to be right in front of us, for all to see, impossible to overlook, no matter where we went.

Although we faced skepticism, it only served to strengthen our conviction to make our dream a reality. Our school had never won a state title in any sport. We were determined to change that history.

By the time football practice started in late August, we were focused. That sense of direction and unity made us a closer team. From day one we gave more in practice and paid more attention to detail as we executed assignments sharply. With our goal imprinted in our minds and hearts, we marched through the season undefeated and stepped into the playoffs with a sense of destiny.

The first playoff game matched us against a

powerhouse team that was riding a 28-game winning streak. We knew we were in for a fight, but, as the intensity of the game increased, so did our determination. We won, pulling away in the second half. That win brought us to the brink of our goal, a match-up with the defending state champions for the title.

We went into preparing for the big game with the same calm intensity and focus we'd shown as a team all season. Then it started to snow. A huge storm blew through that affected the whole state. School was canceled; roads were closed; transportation systems shut down. Still, somehow every member of the team made it to the school gym, and we practiced for the biggest game of our lives in tennis shoes.

Our coach received a phone called before practice the night before the game telling us that state officials were thinking of canceling the game and declaring both teams co-champions because of the severe weather. We were asked if we would accept such a decision.

"No way," was our response. This was our year.

We were not going to get this close and not take a shot at the title.

On Saturday, we arrived at the stadium to find the field buried in snow. The goal posts stuck out above a six to eight inch blanket of snow. Someone asked if snowshoes would be allowed as legal equipment. Undaunted we dressed for the game and began our warm-ups.

Frustration grew as both teams struggled to a scoreless first half. Slips, slides, falls, dropped passes, missed blocks and fumbles were all either team had accomplished. There was a growing sense of urgency that time was running out on our dream.

In the locker room at halftime, Coach Reagan reminded us of all we had been through to get to this moment. Then he reached in his pocket and pulled out the card. Right there in front of us once again was our vision.

"Do you want this?" he asked. Playing conditions were as tough the second half as they were the first, but our determination didn't numb out with our fingers and feet. We scored 34 points in the second half on the same field we couldn't score any on in the first half. Our year-long dream became reality:

"BOONVILLE PIRATES 1974 STATE CHAMPIONS"

And yes, I still have my card.

If you want it—go for it. If you decide to change your mind later, that's all right. You will still be miles ahead of people who refuse to try anything.

One obstacle you are likely to run in to when pursuing your dreams is toxic people.

I once went out to buy a new car. As I drove by a local car dealership, a bright red sports car caught my eye. As I looked it over, I fell in love with the car and knew I had to have it. The price was a little steep, but considering all the accessories the car was equipped with, I thought the price was fair. Suddenly, a salesman appeared to assist with the sale. When he found out that I was a public school teacher, he immediately tried to dissuade me from buying the expensive sports car and redirect me to a more moderately priced model. He was very persistent, trying to convince me that I would be more happy with the lower priced car based on my income.

Finally, I ended the conversation and left the dealership in disgust.

A few days later, I drove by the same dealership and again noticed that shiny red sports car. Once again, I pulled over and admired it. I knew in my heart that this was the car I wanted. Suddenly, another salesman appeared. This salesman was different than the first one. He asked me if I liked the car. My response was a definite "Yes!" He then tossed me the keys and told me to take it out for a spin. Within hours the car was mine.

Knowing what your goals are makes you more prepared to face life's challenges. I often ask my students, "What kind of car do you want to drive?" You will find people in life who will try to compromise your dreams. Some will tell you they are just doing what is best for you. Some, unfortunately, will do it because they don't want to see you succeed. Either way it is not their place.

Your dreams belong to you and no one else. Sometimes dreams are costly. I have found that the best dreams in life come with a price. If you are willing to pay that price, then go for it. I drove that pricy sports car for many years. I never regretted buying it because I loved the car.

Don't settle for second best in life. You deserve the best. What kind of car do you want to drive?

Ode to the Champions

Who are these people,
these doers of deeds,
these dreamer of dreams
who make us believe?
Who are these people
who still win the day
when the odds are against them
and strength fades away?
These people are CHAMPIONS,
for they never give in.
A heart beats within them
that is destined to win.
They follow their dreams,
though the journey seems far.
From the top of a mountain,
they reach out for a star.
And when they have touched it,
when their journey is done,
they give to us hope
from the victories they've won.
So here's to the CHAMPIONS—
to all their great deeds.
They followed their hearts
and became winners indeed.

Tom Krause

My Journaling

Express your thoughts

Chapter 11
Choose Your Reactions

Early in life we learn that sometimes in order to overcome obstacles we must persevere. Perseverance is what makes us "hang in there" and not give up until the problem is solved.

When teens feel they have no control over their lives, they begin to feel powerless. Feelings of apathy lead to feelings of worthlessness. Again, they stop trying and resign themselves to becoming victims of circumstances. Teens need to learn that while they cannot always control events that happen to them – they can control how they react. Their reactions are totally in their control. How they react determines their ultimate outcomes in life.

When you first attempted walking, you fell down a lot. Even though bumps and bruises started to appear, you were determined to keep trying. Soon you were running across the floor.

Stacking was another thing you probably liked

to do. First it was blocks, then it was cans. You learned a lot with your toy blocks by taking your time carefully stacking one block on top of the other. Sometimes the blocks would all fall down. Then you would start over, determined to accomplish your goal of stacking all the blocks.

Though this may sound like a meaningless childhood game, you were learning a good lesson about life. When stacking blocks, you spent a lot of time putting things into place only to see them tumble down around you. It was frustrating! Sometimes you felt like swatting everything away. But after calming down, you began rebuilding, one block at a time. When you finally succeeded, the smile on your face reflected the newfound confidence in yourself.

Winning in life is no more than re-stacking your blocks each time they fall. Persevering until your goal is accomplished and learning to handle adversity are traits that allowed you to find success.

One summer I was waiting for a plane in the Fort Myers, Florida Airport. I noticed a sign across the street, which read: Thomas Edison's Summer

Workshop – Tours Daily. With three hours to kill before my flight, I decided to walk across the street and take the tour.

After paying the fee, I found myself with the rest of the tour party standing in a dark, musty room. The only light came from eight dimly lit bulbs, which hung from the ceiling. As the tour guide entered she explained our environment.

"Look by the wall – what do you see?" she asked.

Peering at the wall I noticed what looked like hundreds of old burned out light bulbs in baskets.

"Those burned out bulbs are all the failed attempts Thomas Edison and his assistants experienced while attempting to invent the light bulb. The eight bulbs still burning are his successful attempts that are still burning today."

Legend has it that after 100 failed attempts, one of Edison's assistants pleaded with him to give up on the idea. "We have tried 100 times, Mr. Edison. It just can't be done,' the assistant explained.

"We have just tried 100 times the wrong way,"

Edison replied. "Change something. It will work.'"

After hundreds of failed attempts, Thomas Edison invented the light bulb. Had it not been for perseverance, it would never had happened.

If you have an idea that you believe in – keep trying. Remember, setbacks don't mean failure. Change something, then keep trying. Nothing great is ever achieved without perseverance.

If you have ever sprained your ankle, you understand pain. After spraining an ankle, you do not want to put any weight on it. All you feel like doing is sitting down and staying off of it. That is exactly what you should do. Put ice on it and stay off it until it starts to heal.

After a few days however, the ankle needs to start being stretched to loosen up the stiffness. When you first get back on the ankle, the tenderness is a quick reminder of the pain experienced during the initial sprain. There is a temptation to not get back on your feet - to stay down and avoid feeling the hurt again. This moment is a turning point in your recovery. If the adhesions are not loosened, the ankle may not heal correctly. You could walk with a limp you whole life.

    In much the same way, life is about overcoming pain and moving towards the future. When bad things happen to people, they feel pain. At that point, they need to take some time to heal. There comes a day, however, when they also need to start on the road to recovery. At that time, it is scary. Many people fear the pain of getting hurt again. This fear may cause them to choose to "sit out" and be a victim the rest of their lives. Others choose to face the pain. What they find is that while there may be a little tenderness at first, the more they get back into life the more they get back to normal. Eventually, instead of going through life with a limp, they are able to run free again.

When Life Hands You the Ball

What will you do – how will you act –
when hurdles stand so tall? Will you rise up and do
your best when backed against a wall?

Will you give up when filled with doubt,
or will you give your all?
The choice is yours – you'll get your chance
when life hands you the ball.

If you're prepared to face each test –
to answer every call –
You'll hold your future in your hands –
seldom will you fall.

And never will the forces win
that make you feel so small.
At last - someday you'll find your dreams
when life hands you the ball.

My Journaling

Express your thoughts

Chapter 12
Relationships: Can I Trust You?

Relationships are important. While you may never use geometry after high school, what you learn about relationships will be useful your whole life. You will always be in some type of relationship. Learning to deal with relationships can be tricky. There is nothing more important than a good friend. There is nothing more damaging than a bad one. Some relationships make you feel wonderful; some make you feel lousy.

All relationships are built on trust. Relationships between parents and teenagers, bosses and employees, friends, siblings, and teammates are all held together by trust. Without this bond, relationships will soon dissolve—especially when adversity strikes.

Trust in a relationship is built over time. People who trust too soon in a relationship sometimes get hurt. This happens a lot in dating relationships. When a dating relationship goes bad, people sometimes feel that they can never trust again. Instead of refusing to trust people, what they should learn is the difference between friends and fleas.

Fleas are parasites. Parasites are organisms that live off other living organisms. When they fail to get what they want from one source, they move on to another. Sometimes people think they have friends, but find out too late that they really had fleas.

People who are only concerned about themselves are called narcissists. Narcissists often expect preferential treatment from others. They expect others to cater (often instantly) to their needs, without being considerate in return. In their mindset, the world revolves around them.

In order for a relationship to be healthy, both parties must find satisfaction. It can't be all one-sided. If you are trying to be friends with someone who always has to have their way, step back and take a good long look. You may be headed for a letdown.

There is a reason most people only have one or two close friends. It is hard to find people you can count on in life. Popularity and friendship are two different things. Remember that if you really want a relationship that lasts, the first thing you need is trust.

Not only should you make sure that you can trust your friends, but you should make sure that others can trust you too. One of the greatest assets a person can develop is trustworthiness. I tell teens all the time, "You will go a lot further in life on trust than looks." If I owned a business, I would hire employees, not based on looks, but on whether they could be counted on to do the job. Being dependable is more valuable to me than anything else. I don't care if you were the homecoming queen; if I couldn't trust you to be at work on time and get your work done, I would have to let you go. On the other hand, I wouldn't care if you were a high school dropout. If I could depend on you, I would not only keep you, but you would be the first employee I would give a raise.

But what if someone lets you down, or you let someone else down? Is the relationship over? Not necessarily. "In order to accept yourself, first you must learn to forgive yourself" is a wise saying. Forgiving yourself for faults or mistakes is a virtue. The same wisdom applies when it comes to relationships. Like you, all people have flaws. Even your best friends will sometimes let you down. When they are truly sorry, learn to forgive. Keep in mind the words of Alexander Pope: "To err is human; to forgive, divine."

What if you feel like you don't have any good friends? Trying to meet new people can be hard, but don't just sit around waiting for people to introduce themselves to you. There are lots of wonderful people you haven't met yet. Don't be put-off be outward appearances. People who seem quiet can be outrageously funny once you get to know them. People who seem shallow can turn-out to be quite thoughtful once you really start talking to them.

Self-trust is a part of relationship building that often goes unnoticed. Part of self-trust is trusting your own judgment over that of others when it comes to relationships. Your opinion matters most. No matter what your friends may think, it is important that you decide who is right for you.

I have known many teens who quickly judge others and enter relationships based only on what their friends think. Sometimes this gets them into bad relationships or prevents them from entering good ones. Remember, trust yourself first before entering a relationship. If you want to get to know new people, be proactive. Go introduce yourself to others. Let them get to know the great person you
are.

The Person That is Me

If ever you should meet me,
the image you may see
is just a mere reflection
of the person that is me.
The person I am really,
the one down deep inside,
is made of many feelings,
which I sometimes try to hide:
feelings of doubt and worry,
of *How will I fit in?*
feelings of hope and longing
that someday I might win;
feelings of frustration
for answers I don't know;
feelings for my loved ones,
relationships that grow.
So remember when you meet me,
the image you may see
is just a mere reflection
of the person that is me.

Tom Krause

My Journaling

Express your thoughts

Chapter 13
Addiction: Keep Your Eyes Open

Why do teenagers take drugs? Answer: Because drugs work. Alcohol and drugs make people feel better. The problem is not only do they take away pain, if you get too deep into drugs they will also take away your future hopes and dreams and eventually your life.

Zack and Trisha met in college. After dating for two years, they decided to get married once they graduated. They were so happy. Filled with dreams, they eagerly awaited their life together.

After the wedding, they both found jobs and bought a small house in a growing community. Time passed, and life was good.

One day Zack was invited to play on the company softball team. Zack enjoyed the time he spent with his colleagues. Several nights a week, Zack spent long hours playing ball and hanging out for a few beers after the games. At first Trisha went with Zack, but after a while, she grew bored and decided to stay home.

Being home alone was not good. Trisha missed Zack's company so she urged him to give up playing softball. Zack refused. He had become accustomed his night out and hated to give up his freedom. An argument took place. Zack agreed not to give up softball all together but to cut back on the amount of nights away.

The following year, Baby Summer was born. Zack and Trisha were so happy. As time went by, the stress of parenthood started to show on Trisha. Now, after work, she was responsible for not only her usual household chores but also for taking care of Summer.

Trisha again went to Zack and urged him to give up softball. She needed help. Zack again balked. Again, an argument arose. Finally, Zack agreed that, instead of playing softball, he would just stop by the local sports bar with his buddies on the way home from work.

A year later, Baby Cody was born. Baby Cody was not the quiet baby that Summer was. Baby Cody was a brat. Constantly crying and demanding attention, Baby Cody brought a tremendous amount of stress to the home. Trisha pleaded for more help around the house from Zack. Zack knew he needed more to help him cope with the stress of work and home. On his way home from work he decided to stop by the liquor store and buy a six-pack of beer to drink on his drive. He also turned to marijuana for his drive home to mellow him out for the stress he would face upon arriving home.

For a while this worked, but not for long; Trisha got tired of Zack coming home at night only to spend his time wasted in the living room chair in front of the television. Another argument occurred.

Zack knew Trisha was right but didn't know what to do. Then Zack was introduced to a new drug by a coworker. Zack discovered that taking crack gave him energy. But crack made Zack different. Instead of just coping with stress, Zack now felt the energy to meet it head on. Now when he came home, instead of

being laidback, Zack was aggressive. He would yell and scare the children. He became loud and threatening, determined to control the chaos in his stressful house. Zack even became physically abusive with Trisha and
the kids.

One day Trisha had enough. She told Zack to never bring crack into the house. Had this been the old laidback Zack, he might have listened to Trisha. But this was a new Zack who wasn't going to listen. Trisha gave Zack an ultimatum: crack or his family. Zack chose crack.

Arriving home from work one day, Zack found his family gone—moved out. Zack didn't care. He still had his beer, marijuana, and crack to keep him happy. He just figured someday they would come to their senses and move back.

Time passed, and they never returned. Zack tried to call Trisha, but she refused to speak to him until the drugs were gone. Zack refused to give them up. Months turned to years, and Zack never relented.

One night, about closing time at a local bar, Zack ran into a new friend. There, sitting next to him, was Ashley. They talked, and Zack discovered they had a lot in common. Ashley liked all the drugs Zack liked. Ashley's family had walked out on her too. Not wanting to be alone any longer, Zack invited Ashley to move in with him. She accepted.

As time passed, Zack noticed that while every morning he went to work to supply money for his lifestyle, Ashley never went to work. She just stayed home and used. Zack finally insisted that Ashley find a job. Ashley promised to get a job but never did. One day, when Zack came home from work, he found that Ashley had moved out and taken all his drugs with her.

Sitting alone in his apartment, Zack thought about calling Trisha. Then Zack realized that he couldn't because Trisha had remarried years ago and moved on with her life. He thought about calling his daughter, Summer. He had heard that she was getting married,

but since he hadn't gotten an invitation, he decided it wouldn't be wise to call her either. Zack read about his son, Cody, in the local sports page. He was running touchdowns for the high school team on Friday nights. Zack had heard, however, that Cody was now calling
another man "Dad," so he decided not to call him either.

Zack is now forty-years-old and alone. He wonders what went wrong.

NO ONE STARTS OUT TO BE ADDICTED BUT IT HAPPENS. Some drugs may seem harmless but others such as opioids are killing people everyday.

Samantha was a cheerleader her sophomore year in high school. She was a happy caring friend. During the end of the school year she was in a car accident which resulted in her breaking her back. Samantha could no longer be a cheerleader and lost most of her friends. She eventually became addicted to the painkillers she was prescribed for her back pain. Life for Samantha began to spiral down hill.

After high school Samantha told her mother, Julie she needed help. She eventually checked into a in-patient rehabilitation facility to get clean. One month into her rehabilitation, Samantha was told she had to leave rehabilitation because insurance would no longer cover her. She told her mother she was not ready to leave. Eight days later Samantha died from an overdose of Opiods. Samantha was twenty years old. A tragic loss of a beautiful girl.

I would be remiss if I didn't mention addiction in a book for teenagers. Teenagers, by nature, experiment with life. But when experimenting goes too far, disaster strikes.

There are two ways to become addicted: physically and psychologically. Physical addiction is when a chemical enters the body and the person becomes hooked on it. Drugs and alcohol are physically addictive. Psychological addiction is when a person becomes obsessed with a thought or idea. Gambling and pornography are examples of addictions that, while not physical, are just as destructive to people and just as hard to break.

If you or your friends are becoming addicted, it is crucial to get help before the disease goes too far. There are many support systems and services available through most schools and/or communities. Don't be afraid to reach out before it is too late. The warning about addiction I give you I learned as a boy: *You've got to know the devil when he is looking you in the eyes.*

I grew up in a small town by a river. At night, old men would cast out bank lines into the river and lie by the river drinking wine until they passed out. In the morning, they would pull in the lines to see if they caught anything. If they did, they would take it to a small market by the river and sell their catch for money to buy more booze.

When I was young, my friends and I would ride our bikes to that market during the summer to buy strawberry soda. The old men who had just sold their fish would sit by the store and try to scare us just for fun. One thing they always said to us was "You got to know the devil when he is looking you in the eyes." Then they would scream and laugh.

One day I decided to not back down from the bullies. When they hollered, I stood still and demanded, "What do you mean—the devil looking you in the eyes?"

"What do you think the devil is going to look like?" one of the men responded. "Do you think he is going to be red and scary looking?" The old man paused a moment, watching me. "No," he said, finally. "He is going to look like your best friend. He is going to make you laugh and have a great time. Then he is going to take your soul."

I understood that the old man was talking about addiction. He knew the trap that lies ahead when drug and alcohol experimentation go awry. His message was a warning from his own life experience. If you ever become tempted by drugs, alcohol, pornography, or something else you know is dangerously addictive, remember: *You've got to know the devil when he is looking you in the eyes.*

Choices

Some people sit—some people try.
Some people laugh—some people cry.
Some people will—some people won't.
Some people do—some people don't.
Some people believe and develop a plan.
Some people doubt—never think that they can.
Some people face hurdles and give them their best.
Some people back down when faced with a test.
Some people complain of their miserable lot.
Some people are thankful for all that they've got.
And when it's all over, when it comes to an end,
some people lose out and some people win.
We all have a choice—we all have a say.
We are spectators in life or we get in and play.
Whichever we choose, however we handle life's game,
the choices are ours; no one else is to blame.

My Journaling

Express your thoughts

Chapter 14
You Have a Purpose

Once upon a time there was a seed that lay upon the ground. The outer shell of the seed was very hard and solid. It protected the inside of the seed from anything on the outside. Time went by, but the seed never changed. After a while, the seed felt useless and wondered what its purpose was.

One day a caring farmer noticed the seed. Carefully, the farmer planted the seed in the ground. Soon it began to rain. As the water seeped through the ground over the seed, its hard shell softened and cracked. The crack allowed the water and other nutrients from the soil to enter inside the seed.

Then a marvelous thing happened—the seed began to grow.
A sprout sprang from the inside of the seed. Slowly, he sprout struggled to work its way to the surface of the ground. As the sprout grew, it began to develop roots, which allowed more water and nutrients to

enter the seed. When the sprout reached the surface, it broke through the ground. Light from the sun burst upon the sprout, causing it to grow even faster than before. Finally, the sprout grew into a vibrant blooming flower. The beautiful color of the flower brought happiness to many people who walked by it on their daily travels. Now the seed knew its purpose.

Does life have a purpose? Is there a plan for all of us? Many people wonder about those questions as they go through life. I can tell you with absolute certainty the answer is yes. Your purpose in life is to share those gifts and talents hidden inside you with others. Your journey in life is to find out what those gifts are and how to share them.

I can tell you what your purpose is, but it is your job to find out the rest. I will give you a hint. Follow the things that interest you. There is a reason you are interested in them. It may not make sense right now, but someday your interest will lead you to your destiny.

I went to college to become a health teacher and coach. While in college, I started taking a lot of classes in speech communication. I don't know why, they just seemed interesting to me. When I graduated from college, I had two majors: one in health/PE and the other in speech communication. For twenty-five years I taught health/PE and never used my speech communication degree. Then I became a professional speaker and have since traveled the world talking to teenagers.

A simple formula for success is "Do what you love, get good at it, and then give it away." Learning to share helps you to feel that your life has a purpose. A fulfilled life is a far greater reward than financial gain. Remember, happiness cannot be measured in money. Happiness is measured in your heart.

As you travel through your teenage years, walk your own path. It will lead you to your purpose. Don't be too hard on yourself, but at the same time, go for your dreams. Whatever interests you is the key to unlocking your future. I don't care if it is biology or auto mechanics; you walk your own life. As you travel your path, one by one the pieces of the puzzle will fall into place, and you will understand why you are here and where you are going.

Being a teenager is huge right now, but pimples aren't permanent. You won't be a teenager your whole life. You will leave this moment behind and walk to your destiny. As you walk, smile and love yourself because you deserve it. You will make it, and when you do, you will look back and see that you were still a work in progress.

I wish you all the best on your walk and pray that someday you also will pass on the lessons you learn in life to future generations of children, whether your own or simply those you meet who could benefit from your love and wisdom.

Becoming

You are on your way to becoming
the person you were meant to be.
Have faith as you go on your journey,
though the end may be so hard to see.
If you feel you are losing direction—
that your footsteps are losing their way—
let your heart be the guide
that will lead you
to keep you from going astray.
Remember, God always is with you—
if ever you should need a friend—
to help with the burdens you carry
and guide you to peace in the end.

Conclusion

The answer to the two questions most teenagers ask themselves: "Am I normal?" and "Will I make it?" is yes. When that little voice in your head tells you anything different—change the message. Remind yourself that you are lovable and capable and that in God's eyes you have worth.

The goal of this book is to give you hope and encouragement as you navigate your teenage years. While this can be a confusing time especially in today's world, you will make it. What you learn about yourself and others during this time will help shape your attitudes for life. It is a time of great change. As you go through your journey, keep in mind that your teenage years are not the end of your changing, but the beginning. You are a work in progress that will someday bloom into a beautiful adult.

It is my prayer that the wisdom in this book helps you in your journey towards a beautifully imperfect and unique life.

Always remember, You Don't Have To Be Perfect and You Will Make it!

About the Author

Tom Krause has been an educator and coach in the Missouri public school system for over twenty years. He is the author *Touching Hearts— Teaching Greatness, The Little Boy's Smile, Who Takes Care of the Caretaker?* and a contributing author to many books in the Chicken Soup for the Soul series as well as several leadership, business, and education magazines.

Tom is also an international motivational speaker whose inspirational. humorous and heartwarming presentations have been enjoyed by audiences worldwide. His presentation, YOU MAKE A DIFFERENCE! is a favorite conference keynote for thousands of audience members.

To learn more about Tom, or to book him for your school district or conference, check online at www.coachkrause.com or Google: Tom Krause motivational speaker for more information.

Tom Krause

Made in the USA
Columbia, SC
12 May 2018